The Essential Highlights from Lovely One Workbook

Applying Ketanji Brown Jackson's Insights to Your Everyday Experience

Dann von

Any resemblance to real events or persons, living or dead, is purely coincidental unless stated otherwise. The insights and exercises provided within this workbook are based on the author's interpretation and should not be taken as professional advice.

First Edition
Published by [Dann von], 2024.

Disclaimer

This workbook, *The Essential Takeaways from Lovely One Workbook: Applying Ketanji Brown Jackson's Life Lessons to Personal Growth*, is an independent resource created to enhance your understanding and application of the concepts presented in *Lovely One: A Memoir* by Ketanji Brown Jackson. It is not the original book and should not be considered a substitute for the original work.

This workbook provides a personal interpretation of the ideas and themes from *Lovely One: A Memoir* and is designed to complement the original text. To fully appreciate the context and content discussed, we encourage readers to refer to the official book by Ketanji Brown Jackson.

Table of content

6. Lessons in Leadership and Inspiring Future Generations

Chapter 1: Introduction to Ketanji Brown Jackson's Life and Legacy

Introduction

Justice Ketanji Brown Jackson stands as a beacon of hope, resilience, and achievement for people everywhere, particularly for those who strive to break barriers in spaces that have historically excluded them. Her appointment as the first Black woman to serve on the United States Supreme Court is not only a personal triumph but a symbol of progress toward a more inclusive and representative society. Her memoir, *Lovely One*, offers readers an intimate glimpse into her life, from her family's legacy of perseverance during segregation to her remarkable ascent to one of the most prestigious and impactful positions in the world of law.

This chapter explores the early life of Ketanji Brown Jackson, the influences that shaped her, and the profound legacy she has built through her personal and professional journey. By delving into her upbringing, education, and early aspirations, readers gain insight into the foundational experiences that set the stage for her rise to the Supreme Court. We also look at her identity as the "Lovely One," the meaning of her name, and how this identity has guided her actions and ambitions throughout her life.

Chapter Summaries

Justice Jackson's memoir can be seen as more than just a story about personal achievement; it's a reflection on what it means to persevere and thrive in the face of adversity. As the first Black woman on the U.S. Supreme Court, her story carries immense cultural and historical significance. Her journey offers inspiration to individuals from all walks of life, especially to those who may feel as though their dreams are too grand for the world to accept. Ketanji's story shows that no dream is too big when it is paired with resilience, determination, and self-belief.

Her memoir, *Lovely One*, also offers a candid reflection on her experiences as a daughter, student, wife, mother, and ultimately, as a trailblazing jurist. Through her reflections, Jackson emphasizes the importance of staying true to one's roots and identity, even while navigating spaces that may not always feel welcoming or inclusive. Her life stands as proof that change is possible, and her memoir carries this powerful message to those who follow in her footsteps.

Key Themes and Ideas

One of the central themes of Ketanji Brown Jackson's life, as highlighted in her memoir, is the idea of legacy and heritage. From an early age, Ketanji understood the importance of where she came from and how her ancestors' experiences of segregation and struggle helped shape her opportunities and worldview. The book highlights the pride Ketanji takes in her family's history and how that pride has fueled her ambition and strengthened her resolve to excel in her chosen path.

Another key theme is the perseverance and determination necessary to overcome obstacles. Justice Jackson's life is a testament to the idea that dreams can be realized even in the face of significant challenges. Whether those challenges involve racial discrimination, economic hardship, or balancing a demanding career with family life, her story demonstrates that success is attainable with resilience and a clear sense of purpose.

Moreover, Ketanji Brown Jackson's memoir touches on the importance of community and mentorship. Throughout her journey, she has been surrounded by mentors and supporters who believed in her potential and encouraged her to aim high. Her experiences illustrate how crucial it is for individuals to have access to mentors who can offer guidance, encouragement, and opportunities for growth.

Critical Analysis

Justice Jackson's life story invites readers to reflect on the power of representation in positions of authority. As the first Black woman to sit on the Supreme Court, her very presence challenges the traditional norms of who gets to be a decision-maker in the highest court of the land. Her story highlights the importance of diversity, not just in terms of race and gender, but also in terms of perspective and lived experience. Her appointment signals a shift in the judicial landscape, one that opens the door for more inclusive decision-making and a broader understanding of justice.

Justice Jackson's journey also invites a deeper reflection on the personal sacrifices often required to achieve professional success. She discusses the challenges of balancing her career with her roles as a wife and mother, and the pressures that come with being a trailblazer in her field. Her candid discussion of these sacrifices offers readers a nuanced view of what it means to "have it all," and the trade-offs that come with pursuing a demanding career.

Reflective Questions

1. How did Ketanji Brown Jackson's family history shape her worldview and her approach to her career?
2. What role did mentorship and community support play in her journey to the Supreme Court?
3. How has Justice Jackson's appointment changed the conversation around diversity in the legal profession and in American society at large?
4. What are the personal sacrifices she made on her path to success, and how did she navigate those challenges?
5. How can we apply lessons from her journey to our own personal and professional challenges?

Practical Applications

Ketanji Brown Jackson's story can serve as a source of motivation and encouragement for individuals facing their own obstacles. Readers can apply her lessons on perseverance and resilience to their own lives, whether they are pursuing educational goals, advancing in their careers, or facing personal challenges. Jackson's commitment to her values, despite the odds, can inspire readers to remain focused on their own long-term goals, even in the face of adversity.

Justice Jackson's story also underscores the importance of seeking out mentorship and building strong support systems. Whether in school, in the workplace, or in personal life, finding mentors who can offer guidance and encouragement is crucial to long-term success. Readers can use Jackson's experiences as a reminder to cultivate relationships that will support their growth and development.

Character Profiles (if applicable)

- **Ketanji Brown Jackson**: The central figure of the memoir, Jackson's journey from a young girl with dreams of success to her appointment to the U.S. Supreme Court is chronicled in detail. Her story is one of resilience, determination, and a commitment to justice.
- **Her Parents**: Jackson's parents, both educators, played a significant role in shaping her sense of identity and purpose. Their commitment to education and their pride in their heritage provided a strong foundation for Jackson's own success.
- **Her Mentors**: Throughout her career, Jackson benefited from

the guidance of mentors who saw her potential and encouraged her to reach for greater heights.

Author's Vision and Purpose

Ketanji Brown Jackson wrote *Lovely One* to share her personal story with the world, but also to provide a source of inspiration for future generations. Her memoir serves as a reminder that success is possible, even in spaces that have historically excluded people who look like her. Her vision is one of hope and possibility, and she encourages readers to believe in their own potential to effect change in their lives and communities.

Key Quotes and Insights

- "I stand on the shoulders of those who came before me, those who paved the way so that

I could dream big and achieve even bigger."
- "It is not enough to succeed for oneself; true success comes when we lift others up along the way."
- "Justice is not just a concept; it is an action, one that requires perseverance and courage."

Personal Takeaways

Readers of *Lovely One* will walk away with a deeper understanding of the power of perseverance and the importance of staying true to one's values. Jackson's story is a testament to the fact that no matter the challenges we face, we can achieve great things with determination, support, and a clear vision of what we want to accomplish.

Action Steps and Implementation

To apply the lessons from Jackson's life to your own, consider setting clear goals for yourself, just as she did from a young age. Seek out mentors who can help you along the way, and stay true to your values, even when the path ahead seems difficult. Remember, success is not just about personal achievement, but about creating opportunities for others as well.

Final Reflections

Justice Ketanji Brown Jackson's life and legacy are a testament to the power of perseverance, resilience, and the importance of representation. Her story serves as a source of inspiration for all who read it, reminding us that we can achieve greatness no matter where we come from or what obstacles we face.

Further Reading and Resources

- *My Beloved World* by Sonia Sotomayor
- *Becoming* by Michelle Obama
- *Just Mercy* by Bryan Stevenson
- Various articles on Justice Ketanji Brown Jackson's legal rulings and public service.

Chapter 2: Family Heritage and Overcoming Barriers

Introduction

Ketanji Brown Jackson's story is not just about her individual accomplishments; it is deeply rooted in her family's history and heritage. Her family's journey from the segregated South to positions of influence and education forms the bedrock of her identity and values. Understanding her family's legacy is crucial to understanding the determination and drive that propelled her to break through barriers that have historically excluded people of color from positions of power, particularly in the legal field.

In this chapter, we will explore the rich heritage that Ketanji inherited from her ancestors, her parents' significant influence on her personal and professional development, and how their experiences with segregation and perseverance shaped her approach to her career and life. This chapter also examines the ways in which she internalized their legacy of resilience and used it as a foundation to overcome systemic obstacles, charting a path that ultimately led her to the Supreme Court.

Chapter Summaries

Ketanji Brown Jackson's family history is a microcosm of the larger story of Black resilience and achievement in America. Her grandparents and parents lived through segregation, with her grandparents facing harsh racial discrimination in the segregated South. Her parents, Johnny and Ellery Brown, were born in the mid-1940s and grew up during the Civil Rights Movement. They were among the first generation of African Americans to fully integrate into mainstream American institutions after the formal end of segregation.

Johnny Brown became the chief attorney for the Miami-Dade County School Board, and Ellery Brown was a school principal. Both were educators who placed a premium on education and instilled in their daughter a sense of pride in her heritage and the importance of perseverance. The name "Ketanji Onyika," which means "Lovely One" in West African languages, was a deliberate choice by her parents to ground her in her cultural roots and to remind her of her heritage's beauty and strength.

This family legacy of resilience and overcoming barriers has deeply influenced Ketanji's outlook on life.

She grew up with an awareness of the struggles her ancestors endured and with a clear sense of duty to honor their legacy by excelling in her own pursuits. Ketanji's story is thus interwoven with the larger narrative of African American history, and her achievements reflect both her personal resolve and the generational progress her family represents.

Key Themes and Ideas

A central theme in Ketanji Brown Jackson's family history is the idea of **breaking barriers**. Her grandparents and parents faced institutionalized racism and were among the pioneers of integration in education and the workforce. Their perseverance in the face of discrimination was not just about surviving—it was about excelling and opening doors for future generations. Ketanji inherited this determination and has carried it forward in her own career, consistently pushing past obstacles to reach new heights.

Another key theme is **the importance of education**. Ketanji's parents were educators who believed deeply in the transformative power of education. They emphasized the importance of academic achievement from a young age and provided Ketanji with the support and encouragement she needed to excel. This belief in education as a tool for social mobility and personal empowerment became a core value in Ketanji's life.

Finally, the theme of **family legacy** is central to Ketanji's story. She did not achieve her success in isolation; rather, her accomplishments are part of a larger narrative of family progress. Her grandparents' and parents' sacrifices and successes laid the groundwork for Ketanji to pursue her dreams, and she remains deeply aware of her role in carrying forward their legacy.

Critical Analysis

Ketanji Brown Jackson's family history serves as a powerful reminder of the impact that generational progress can have on an individual's opportunities and outlook. Her story highlights the ways in which systemic barriers can be overcome through perseverance, education, and a strong sense of identity. The legacy of her grandparents and parents is not just a backdrop to her achievements—it is a driving force that has shaped her entire approach to life and law.

Her family's experience also underscores the idea that individual success is often the result of collective effort. Ketanji's accomplishments are built on the foundation of her ancestors' struggles and triumphs. This interconnectedness between past and present is a key aspect of her story, and it challenges the notion that success is purely an individual pursuit. Instead, her story demonstrates that success is often the culmination of efforts that span generations.

Moreover, Ketanji's life illustrates the importance of **representation** in positions of power. Her grandparents and parents worked within segregated and often hostile environments, and their achievements paved the way for Ketanji to reach the Supreme Court. Her success is not just personal—it is a symbol of progress for all those who have been historically excluded from such positions.

Reflective Questions

1. How did Ketanji Brown Jackson's family history influence her approach to overcoming obstacles in her personal and professional life?
2. What role did education play in Ketanji's development, and how did her parents' emphasis on education shape her career?
3. In what ways does Ketanji's story reflect the broader experience of African American progress in the face of systemic racism?
4. How does Ketanji's achievement on the Supreme Court serve as a continuation of her family's legacy of breaking barriers?
5. How can understanding one's heritage and family history provide strength and motivation in the face of challenges?

Practical Applications

Ketanji Brown Jackson's story encourages readers to reflect on their own family histories and the ways in which their ancestors' experiences have shaped their own opportunities and perspectives. By understanding the sacrifices and achievements of previous generations, individuals can draw strength from their heritage and use it as a source of motivation to overcome their own challenges.

Additionally, Ketanji's emphasis on education as a pathway to success serves as a reminder of the importance of lifelong learning and self-improvement. Readers can apply this lesson to their own lives by seeking out educational opportunities and continuing to invest in their personal growth, regardless of the obstacles they may face.

Character Profiles (if applicable)

- **Johnny and Ellery Brown:** Ketanji's parents, both educators, who instilled in her a love of learning and a deep pride in her heritage. Their achievements in the face of systemic racism laid the groundwork for Ketanji's success.
- **Ketanji Brown Jackson:** The central figure of the memoir, Ketanji's story of breaking barriers is deeply influenced by her family's legacy of perseverance and progress.
- **Ketanji's Grandparents:** Though not as prominently featured in the memoir, their experiences with segregation and racial discrimination are an important part of Ketanji's family history and have shaped her

understanding of justice and equality.

Author's Vision and Purpose

Through *Lovely One*, Ketanji Brown Jackson seeks to honor her family's legacy while also sharing her own journey of breaking barriers and achieving success. Her memoir is not just a personal reflection; it is a celebration of the progress made by African Americans over generations and an invitation to readers to continue striving for excellence in their own lives.

Her purpose is to inspire readers to recognize the power of their own heritage and to use it as a source of strength and motivation. By sharing her story, she hopes to encourage others to pursue their dreams, no matter how daunting the obstacles may seem.

Key Quotes and Insights

- "My name, Ketanji Onyika, means 'Lovely One.' It is a reminder of where I come from and the beauty and strength of my heritage."
- "My parents taught me that education was the key to success, and they made sure I knew that no barrier was insurmountable with hard work and determination."
- "I stand on the shoulders of those who came before me—my grandparents, my parents—who paved the way so that I could dream big and achieve even bigger."

Personal Takeaways

Readers of *Lovely One* will gain a deeper appreciation for the role that family history and heritage can play in shaping one's identity and success.

Ketanji's story is a powerful example of how understanding and embracing one's roots can provide the strength needed to overcome even the most daunting challenges.

Action Steps and Implementation

To apply the lessons from Ketanji's family history, consider exploring your own heritage and the stories of those who came before you. Reflect on how their experiences have shaped your opportunities and use their stories as a source of motivation. Additionally, make education and personal growth a priority in your life, just as Ketanji's parents did for her.

Final Reflections

Ketanji Brown Jackson's family history is a testament to the power of perseverance and the importance of breaking barriers. Her story reminds us that success is often the result of collective effort, and that understanding our own heritage can provide us with the strength and resilience needed to achieve our dreams.

Further Reading and Resources

- *The Warmth of Other Suns* by Isabel Wilkerson
- *Hidden Figures* by Margot Lee Shetterly
- *The Souls of Black Folk* by W.E.B. Du Bois
- Various articles on African American history and the Civil Rights Movement.

Chapter 3: Education and Early Career

Introduction

Ketanji Brown Jackson's academic journey and early career are testaments to the power of determination, hard work, and resilience. From her childhood in Miami, Florida, to her magna cum laude graduation from Harvard University and beyond, her academic excellence and dedication set her on a path to becoming one of the most respected legal minds in the country. This chapter delves into Ketanji's educational experiences, highlighting the challenges she faced as a Black woman in elite academic institutions and how her early career choices helped her build the foundation for her future success.

Ketanji's experiences at Harvard College and Harvard Law School are central to understanding her development, both as a scholar and as a professional. They also reveal her evolving sense of purpose, commitment to justice, and desire to challenge the status quo. We will explore her involvement in academic and extracurricular activities, her professional experiences during law school, and her initial forays into the legal profession that set her on the path to the U.S. Supreme Court.

Chapter Summaries

From a young age, Ketanji Brown Jackson demonstrated a profound passion for education. Growing up in a household where learning was deeply valued, she excelled academically and developed a strong work ethic. After graduating from high school as an honor student and a student body president, she was accepted to Harvard College, where she pursued a degree in government.

Harvard presented both opportunities and challenges for Ketanji. As one of the few Black women in her cohort, she faced the pressures of navigating a predominantly white institution. However, Ketanji was determined to thrive in this environment. She participated in student organizations that amplified the voices of marginalized communities and became known for her intelligence, poise, and activism. During her time at Harvard, Ketanji was also involved in theater and improv, reflecting her multifaceted personality and interests.

After earning her undergraduate degree, Ketanji continued at Harvard Law School, where she faced an even more intense academic environment. However, she thrived despite the challenges, becoming an editor of the prestigious *Harvard Law Review* and gaining invaluable experience through internships and clerkships. Her academic and professional success at Harvard propelled her into a career that included clerking for U.S. Supreme Court Justice Stephen Breyer and serving in roles in both the private and public sectors.

Key Themes and Ideas

One of the central themes of Ketanji Brown Jackson's educational journey is **the power of perseverance**. Despite the numerous obstacles she faced as a Black woman in elite institutions, Ketanji remained steadfast in her commitment to excellence. She encountered both overt and subtle forms of discrimination but used these experiences to fuel her determination to succeed. Her story exemplifies the importance of resilience and staying true to one's goals, even in the face of adversity.

Another key theme is **the importance of community and support.** While at Harvard, Ketanji found strength in the support of her family, friends, and fellow students who shared her experiences as a minority in a predominantly white institution. This sense of community helped her navigate the challenges of higher education and provided her with the emotional and intellectual support she needed to thrive. Ketanji's involvement in student organizations also speaks to her commitment to creating spaces for others like her to feel seen and heard.

A final theme is **the value of a diverse education.** Ketanji's involvement in theater, debate, and student government at Harvard reflects her belief in the importance of a well-rounded education. These activities helped her develop a broad skill set that would serve her well in her legal career. Ketanji's approach to education was not limited to academics; it included a commitment to personal growth, leadership, and creativity.

Critical Analysis

Ketanji Brown Jackson's educational journey illustrates the complexities of being a trailblazer in environments that have historically excluded people of color, particularly Black women. Her experiences at Harvard highlight the ways in which educational institutions can both challenge and support students from underrepresented backgrounds. While Ketanji encountered difficulties related to race and gender, she was able to navigate these challenges by drawing on her inner strength and the support of her community.

Her story also raises important questions about **access to elite education** and the role that institutions play in shaping future leaders. Ketanji's success at Harvard and beyond is a testament to her intelligence and hard work, but it also underscores the importance of creating inclusive environments where all students, regardless of their background, can thrive. Her story challenges educational institutions to consider how they can better support students from diverse backgrounds and ensure that they are not only admitted but also given the tools and opportunities to succeed.

Ketanji's early career choices also reveal her deep commitment to justice and public service. Her decision to clerk for judges, including Justice Breyer, and her work in both private law firms and public institutions, demonstrate her desire to use the law as a tool for positive change. Her career trajectory shows that success in the legal profession is not just about personal achievement—it is about using one's skills and knowledge to serve others and advance justice.

Reflective Questions

1. How did Ketanji Brown Jackson's experiences at Harvard shape her approach to her legal career and her views on justice and equality?
2. What role did community and support play in Ketanji's academic and professional success, and how can individuals create similar

support networks in their own lives?

3. How did Ketanji's involvement in extracurricular activities contribute to her personal and professional development, and what lessons can be drawn from her diverse educational experiences?

4. In what ways do Ketanji's experiences at Harvard reflect the broader challenges faced by minority students in elite educational institutions?

5. How did Ketanji's early career choices reflect her commitment to public service and social justice, and how can these choices inspire others to pursue meaningful careers in law or other fields?

Practical Applications

Ketanji Brown Jackson's educational journey offers several practical lessons for readers. First, her story emphasizes the importance of **perseverance in the face of adversity**. No matter what challenges one faces, remaining committed to one's goals and drawing on personal resilience can lead to success. Readers can apply this lesson by setting clear goals for themselves and remaining focused, even when obstacles arise.

Second, Ketanji's experiences highlight the value of **building strong support networks**. By seeking out mentors, friends, and peers who share similar experiences or goals, individuals can create a sense of community that provides emotional and intellectual support. Readers can apply this lesson by actively seeking out and cultivating relationships with people who inspire and uplift them.

Finally, Ketanji's diverse educational experiences demonstrate the importance of **exploring a wide range of interests**. Readers can apply this lesson by pursuing activities outside of their immediate career goals that allow them to develop new skills and perspectives. This approach to education fosters personal growth and can lead to new opportunities and insights.

Character Profiles (if applicable)

- **Ketanji Brown Jackson**: The protagonist of the memoir, Ketanji's academic and early career experiences reveal her resilience, intelligence, and commitment to justice. Her time at Harvard shaped her views on law, race, and gender, and set her on a path to the Supreme Court.

- **Justice Stephen Breyer:** As one of Ketanji's mentors, Justice Breyer played a significant role in her early legal career. His influence is reflected in Ketanji's approach to law and her dedication to public service.
- **Harvard Community:** The friends, mentors, and fellow students who supported Ketanji during her time at Harvard played a crucial role in helping her navigate the challenges of being a minority student in an elite institution.

Author's Vision and Purpose

Through *Lovely One*, Ketanji Brown Jackson aims to share not only her personal story but also the broader lessons she has learned about perseverance, community, and justice. Her experiences at Harvard and in her early career provide valuable insights for readers seeking to overcome obstacles and achieve success in their own lives. By sharing these stories, Ketanji hopes to inspire others to pursue their dreams, no matter how difficult the journey may seem.

Key Quotes and Insights

- "Harvard taught me many things—most importantly, that I could succeed, even in spaces where people didn't look like me or expect me to thrive."
- "I learned early on that education was my pathway to opportunity, and I was determined to make the most of it."
- "The challenges I faced at Harvard were real, but they also prepared me for the even greater challenges I would face in my legal career."

Personal Takeaways

Readers of *Lovely One* will be inspired by Ketanji's resilience and determination. Her story demonstrates that success is not just about intelligence or talent—it is about perseverance, community, and a commitment to personal growth. Readers will come away with a deeper understanding of how to overcome obstacles and build successful careers, even in the face of adversity.

Action Steps and Implementation

To apply the lessons from Ketanji's educational journey, readers can focus on building strong support networks, pursuing a diverse range of interests, and remaining resilient in the face of challenges. By setting clear goals, seeking out mentors and allies, and maintaining a commitment to personal growth, readers can follow in Ketanji's footsteps and achieve their own dreams.

Final Reflections

Ketanji Brown Jackson's educational and early career experiences offer valuable insights into the power of perseverance, community, and personal growth. Her story is a reminder that success is not always linear, but with the right mindset and support, it is possible to overcome even the most daunting challenges.

Further Reading and Resources

- *Becoming* by Michelle Obama
- *My Own Words* by Ruth Bader Ginsburg
- *The Color of Law* by Richard Rothstein
- Various articles on the experiences of minority students in elite educational institutions.

Chapter 4: Navigating the Legal Profession and Breaking Boundaries

Introduction

Ketanji Brown Jackson's rise through the legal ranks is a story of perseverance, hard work, and a relentless pursuit of justice. As a Black woman in a profession dominated by white men, Ketanji broke barriers at nearly every stage of her career. Her journey to the Supreme Court was not only a personal triumph but also a symbolic victory for underrepresented groups in the legal field. This chapter explores how Ketanji navigated the challenges of the legal profession, from her clerkships to her time as a federal judge, and ultimately her historic appointment to the U.S. Supreme Court.

Ketanji's career path highlights her dedication to public service and her commitment to using the law as a tool for social change. We will examine the key moments in her legal career, the challenges she faced, and the impact she has made on the legal profession. Her story serves as a powerful example of how one individual can break through systemic barriers and create a lasting legacy.

Chapter Summaries

Ketanji Brown Jackson's career began with prestigious clerkships, including a clerkship with U.S. Supreme Court Justice Stephen Breyer, which shaped her understanding of the law and its application. After her clerkships, she worked in private practice, but her passion for public service led her to take on roles in the public sector, including serving as a federal public defender and as Vice Chair of the U.S. Sentencing Commission.

Ketanji's time on the U.S. Sentencing Commission was particularly significant, as she worked to address disparities in federal sentencing, especially in cases involving drug offenses. Her efforts helped to bring about reforms that reduced sentencing disparities between crack and powder cocaine offenses, which disproportionately affected Black Americans. Her work on the commission demonstrated her commitment to fairness and equality in the justice system.

In 2013, Ketanji was appointed to the U.S. District Court for the District of Columbia, where she gained a reputation as a thoughtful and fair judge. Her rulings often reflected her deep understanding of the law and her belief in the importance of civil rights and justice for all. In 2021, President Joe Biden nominated her to the U.S. Court of Appeals for the D.C. Circuit, and just one year later, she made history as the first Black woman to be appointed to the U.S. Supreme Court.

Key Themes and Ideas

One of the central themes of Ketanji Brown Jackson's legal career is **breaking barriers and challenging the status quo**. At every stage of her career, Ketanji faced obstacles related to her race and gender, but she refused to let these barriers define her or limit her success. Her story is a powerful reminder that perseverance and dedication can help individuals overcome systemic challenges and achieve their goals.

Another key theme is **the importance of public service and using the law for social good**. Ketanji's decision to work as a federal public defender and her efforts on the U.S. Sentencing Commission demonstrate her commitment to using the law as a tool for positive change. Throughout her career, she has prioritized fairness, equality, and justice, particularly for marginalized communities.

Finally, Ketanji's career reflects **the value of mentorship and support networks.** Her clerkship with Justice Stephen Breyer played a significant role in shaping her legal philosophy and career trajectory. Throughout her career, Ketanji has benefited from the guidance and support of mentors, and she has also served as a mentor to others. Her story highlights the importance of building strong professional relationships and giving back to the next generation of legal professionals.

Critical Analysis

Ketanji Brown Jackson's career trajectory is a testament to her intelligence, perseverance, and commitment to justice. However, her rise to the Supreme Court also raises important questions about **representation in the legal profession**. The legal field has long been dominated by white men, and Ketanji's success represents a step toward greater diversity and inclusion in the judiciary. Her appointment to the Supreme Court is a powerful symbol of progress, but it also underscores the need for continued efforts to break down barriers for underrepresented groups in the legal profession.

Ketanji's work on the U.S. Sentencing Commission is particularly noteworthy, as it reflects her belief in the importance of **criminal justice**

reform. Her efforts to address sentencing disparities for drug offenses had a significant impact on the lives of countless individuals, particularly in Black and Brown communities. Her work on the commission highlights the role that judges and policymakers can play in addressing systemic injustices and making the legal system more equitable.

At the same time, Ketanji's career raises questions about the **challenges faced by women of color in the legal profession**. Despite her impressive credentials and achievements, Ketanji faced significant obstacles related to her race and gender. Her story highlights the need for continued efforts to create more inclusive environments in the legal field, where individuals from diverse backgrounds can thrive.

Reflective Questions

1. How did Ketanji Brown Jackson's experiences as a public defender and on the U.S. Sentencing Commission shape her views on justice and equality?

2. In what ways has Ketanji's career challenged the status quo in the legal profession, and what impact has her success had on representation in the judiciary?

3. How has mentorship played a role in Ketanji's career, and how can individuals build strong professional networks to support their own success?

4. What lessons can be learned from Ketanji's commitment to public service, and how can individuals use their careers to create positive change in their communities?

5. What challenges do women of color continue to face in the legal profession, and what steps can be taken to create more inclusive environments in the judiciary and beyond?

Practical Applications

Ketanji Brown Jackson's career offers several practical lessons for readers, particularly those interested in pursuing careers in law or public service. First, her story emphasizes the importance of **perseverance in the face of adversity**. Ketanji's success did not come easily, but she remained committed to her goals and refused to let systemic barriers hold her back. Readers can apply this lesson by staying focused on their long-term goals and remaining resilient, even when faced with obstacles.

Second, Ketanji's career highlights the value of **mentorship and professional networks.** Throughout her career, Ketanji benefited from the guidance of mentors like Justice Breyer, and she also made it a priority to mentor others. Readers can apply this lesson by seeking out mentors and building strong professional relationships that can provide support and guidance throughout their careers.

Finally, Ketanji's commitment to **public service and social justice** serves as an inspiration for individuals who want to use their careers to create positive change. Whether working as a public defender, serving on the U.S. Sentencing Commission, or ruling on cases as a judge, Ketanji has consistently prioritized fairness and equality. Readers can apply this lesson by considering how they can use their own careers to make a difference in their communities and advance justice for all.

Character Profiles (if applicable)

- **Ketanji Brown Jackson**: A trailblazer in the legal profession, Ketanji's career reflects her commitment to justice, equality, and public service. Her work as a public defender, judge, and Supreme Court justice demonstrates her belief in the power of the law to create positive change.
- **Justice Stephen Breyer**: As one of Ketanji's mentors, Justice Breyer played a significant role in shaping her legal philosophy and career trajectory. His influence can be seen in Ketanji's approach to the law and her commitment to fairness and equality.

- **Colleagues and Peers:** Throughout her career, Ketanji has worked alongside colleagues and peers who have supported her and helped her navigate the challenges of the legal profession. These individuals have played a crucial role in her success and have contributed to her development as a legal professional.

Author's Vision and Purpose

Through *Lovely One*, Ketanji Brown Jackson aims to share her journey as a Black woman navigating the legal profession and breaking through systemic barriers. Her story is one of perseverance, dedication, and a commitment to justice. By sharing her experiences, Ketanji hopes to inspire others to pursue their dreams and challenge the status quo, no matter the obstacles they face.

Key Quotes and Insights

- "I entered the legal profession knowing that I would face challenges related to my race and gender, but I also knew that my commitment to justice would guide me through."
- "Public service has always been at the heart of my career. Whether as a public defender, a judge, or a Supreme Court justice, my goal has always been to use the law to create a fairer, more just society."
- "Breaking barriers is never easy, but it is necessary. We must continue to push for greater diversity and inclusion in the legal profession and beyond."

Personal Takeaways

Readers of *Lovely One* will be inspired by Ketanji's resilience and determination. Her story demonstrates that success in the legal profession requires not only intelligence and hard work but also a commitment to justice and equality. Readers will come away with a deeper understanding of how to overcome obstacles and create lasting change in their own careers and communities.

Action Steps and Implementation

To apply the lessons from Ketanji's legal career, readers can focus on building strong professional networks, seeking out mentorship, and remaining committed to their goals even in the face of adversity. By staying true to their values and using their skills to advance justice and equality, readers can follow in Ketanji's footsteps and create positive change in their own communities.

Final Reflections

Ketanji Brown Jackson's legal career is a powerful example of how individuals can break barriers and challenge the status quo. Her commitment to public service, justice, and equality serves as an inspiration for all who aspire to make a difference in the world. By sharing her story, Ketanji invites readers to reflect on their own journeys and consider how they can use their careers to create a more just and equitable society.

Further Reading and Resources

- *Sisters in Law* by Linda Hirshman
- *Just Mercy* by Bryan Stevenson
- *The New Jim Crow* by Michelle Alexander
- Various articles on diversity and inclusion in the legal profession.

Chapter 5: Balancing Career, Marriage, and Motherhood

Introduction

Balancing a demanding career with the responsibilities of marriage and motherhood is a challenge that many women face, and Justice Ketanji Brown Jackson's story is no exception. Despite her career in the highest echelons of the legal world, Ketanji has remained deeply committed to her family. This chapter explores how Ketanji navigated the complexities of being a working mother and wife while pursuing her ambitions in the legal profession. We delve into the struggles and triumphs she experienced in managing her professional and personal life, offering insights into the strategies she used to maintain balance and fulfillment.

Justice Ketanji's journey serves as a powerful example for other women who seek to achieve professional success without sacrificing their roles as mothers and partners. Her story underscores the importance of support systems, resilience, and prioritizing self-care in order to thrive both personally and professionally.

Chapter Summaries

Ketanji Brown Jackson's legal career has been marked by numerous achievements, but her success would not have been possible without the strong foundation of her family life. Ketanji married surgeon Patrick Jackson, and together they have two daughters. Despite the challenges of raising a family while navigating a demanding legal career, Ketanji and her husband worked as a team, supporting each other's professional ambitions and sharing the responsibilities of parenting.

As a federal judge, Ketanji often worked long hours, but she made it a priority to be present for her family. She would attend her daughters' school events, help with homework, and create special family traditions. At the same time, Ketanji's career required sacrifices, including missed family moments and the constant challenge of balancing competing demands.

Through it all, Ketanji has been open about the difficulties she faced in trying to "do it all." Her story offers valuable lessons for other working mothers, emphasizing the importance of setting boundaries, seeking support, and recognizing that no one can be perfect in every aspect of life.

Key Themes and Ideas

One of the primary themes of this chapter is **the struggle for work-life balance**. Ketanji's experience illustrates the challenges faced by working mothers who strive to excel in their careers while also being present for their families. Her story emphasizes the importance of finding ways to manage time effectively, delegate responsibilities, and prioritize what matters most.

Another key theme is **the importance of support systems**. Throughout her career, Ketanji has relied on the support of her husband, family, friends, and colleagues. This network of support has allowed her to pursue her career while still being a dedicated mother and wife. Her story highlights the need for strong partnerships and the willingness to seek help when needed.

Additionally, **resilience and self-compassion** are crucial themes in Ketanji's story. She acknowledges that balancing career and family is never easy and that there will be moments of struggle and imperfection. By being kind to herself and recognizing that she cannot be "perfect" in every aspect of her life, Ketanji has been able to maintain her well-being while pursuing her ambitions.

Critical Analysis

Ketanji Brown Jackson's ability to balance her career and family life is a testament to her resilience and determination, but it also raises important questions about **society's expectations of working mothers.** Women in demanding careers are often expected to juggle their professional responsibilities with the duties of motherhood, a challenge that is not always equally shared by men. Ketanji's story underscores the need for **greater equity in caregiving roles** and for societal changes that allow women to pursue their ambitions without being disproportionately burdened by family responsibilities.

At the same time, Ketanji's experience highlights the **structural barriers** that many working mothers face. While she has been able to succeed in her career with the support of her family, other women may not have the same resources or opportunities. Her story raises questions about how workplaces can better support working parents through policies such as flexible work hours, parental leave, and childcare support.

Ketanji's candid reflections on the challenges of balancing career and family also challenge the notion of the "superwoman" myth, which suggests that women can and should be able to excel in all areas of life without difficulty. Her story offers a more realistic and compassionate view of what it means to be a working mother, encouraging women to be kinder to themselves and to seek support when needed.

Reflective Questions

1. How has Ketanji Brown Jackson managed to balance her demanding legal career with the responsibilities of motherhood and marriage?
2. What role has Ketanji's support system played in helping her navigate the challenges of balancing her personal and professional life?
3. What lessons can be learned from Ketanji's experience about setting boundaries and

prioritizing self-care as a working mother?

4. How can workplaces and society better support working mothers in balancing career and family responsibilities?

5. In what ways does Ketanji's story challenge traditional gender roles and expectations for women in the workplace and at home?

Practical Applications

Ketanji Brown Jackson's story offers several practical lessons for readers, particularly those who are juggling the demands of career and family. First, her experience emphasizes the importance of **setting boundaries and prioritizing self-care**. By recognizing that it is impossible to be perfect in every aspect of life, Ketanji has been able to focus on what matters most to her while maintaining her well-being. Readers can apply this lesson by identifying their own priorities and setting boundaries to protect their time and energy.

Second, Ketanji's story highlights the value of **strong support systems**. Whether it is a partner, family members, friends, or colleagues, having a network of support can make it easier to manage the demands of career and family life. Readers can apply this lesson by seeking out and nurturing supportive relationships that can provide assistance and encouragement when needed.

Finally, Ketanji's story encourages readers to **embrace flexibility and adaptability**. Balancing career and family is never a straightforward task, and there will inevitably be moments of struggle and compromise. Readers can apply this lesson by being open to change and by finding creative solutions to the challenges they face.

Character Profiles (if applicable)

- **Ketanji Brown Jackson**: A trailblazing legal professional, Ketanji's ability to balance her career with her roles as a mother and wife serves as an inspiration for other working mothers. Her story reflects resilience, determination, and a commitment to both her family and her professional goals.
- **Patrick Jackson**: Ketanji's husband and a surgeon, Patrick has been a supportive partner throughout her career. Together, they have navigated the challenges of raising a family while pursuing demanding careers, demonstrating the

importance of teamwork and mutual support.

- **Daughters of Ketanji Brown Jackson**: Ketanji's daughters have played a central role in her life, and her commitment to being an involved mother has been a priority despite her demanding career. Her relationship with her daughters reflects her dedication to both her family and her profession.

Author's Vision and Purpose

In this chapter of *Lovely One*, Ketanji Brown Jackson aims to share her personal experience of balancing career, marriage, and motherhood. Her story is a testament to the challenges and rewards of being a working mother, and she hopes to offer insights and encouragement to other women who are navigating similar paths. By sharing her journey,

Ketanji seeks to inspire readers to pursue their professional ambitions while also nurturing their personal lives.

Key Quotes and Insights

- "Balancing career and family is not about perfection; it's about finding what works for you and being kind to yourself along the way."
- "My family is my foundation. They give me the strength and support I need to pursue my career, and they remind me of what truly matters in life."
- "There are days when I feel like I'm not doing enough at work or at home, but I've learned that it's okay to ask for help and to recognize that no one can do it all."

Personal Takeaways

Readers of *Lovely One* will be inspired by Ketanji's honesty and resilience in balancing her career with her roles as a mother and wife. Her story serves as a reminder that it is possible to pursue professional success without sacrificing personal fulfillment. Readers will come away with practical strategies for managing work-life balance and a deeper appreciation for the importance of self-care and support networks.

Action Steps and Implementation

To apply the lessons from Ketanji's experience, readers can focus on creating a **supportive network** of family, friends, and colleagues who can help them manage the demands of career and family life. Additionally, readers can prioritize **self-care and setting boundaries** to ensure that they are not overwhelmed by the pressures of work and home. By embracing flexibility and seeking help when needed, readers can navigate the challenges of balancing their personal and professional lives.

Final Reflections

Ketanji Brown Jackson's story of balancing career, marriage, and motherhood is one of resilience, determination, and grace. Her experience offers valuable lessons for all working parents, encouraging them to seek balance, embrace imperfection, and prioritize what matters most in life. Through her journey, Ketanji demonstrates that it is possible to achieve professional success while still nurturing a fulfilling personal life.

Further Reading and Resources

- *Lean In* by Sheryl Sandberg

- *Overwhelmed: Work, Love, and Play When No One Has the Time* by Brigid Schulte
- *I Know How She Does It* by Laura Vanderkam
- Articles on work-life balance and the challenges faced by working mothers.

Chapter 6: Lessons in Leadership and Inspiring Future Generations

Introduction

Justice Ketanji Brown Jackson's remarkable journey from a young girl with ambitious dreams to a Supreme Court Justice provides a wealth of lessons in leadership. Throughout her career, Ketanji has demonstrated qualities that have not only helped her achieve professional success but also serve as a source of inspiration for future generations. This chapter explores the key lessons in leadership gleaned from Ketanji's experiences and how they can be applied to inspire and guide others.

Ketanji's story illustrates the importance of perseverance, integrity, and vision in leadership. Her ability to navigate challenges, advocate for justice, and maintain a commitment to her values highlights essential leadership principles that are relevant to both personal and professional contexts. By examining her journey, readers can gain insights into effective leadership practices and learn how to inspire and mentor others.

Chapter Summaries

Ketanji Brown Jackson's leadership style is characterized by a commitment to justice, a deep sense of integrity, and a focus on mentorship and empowerment. Her rise to the Supreme Court was not only the result of her legal acumen but also her dedication to leading with empathy and fairness.

Key moments in Ketanji's leadership journey include her work as a public defender, her time as a judge on the U.S. Court of Appeals, and her role as a Supreme Court Justice. Each of these roles required her to demonstrate resilience and a strong sense of justice. Her leadership was evident in her ability to advocate for the rights of others, her fair and thoughtful approach to decision-making, and her dedication to mentoring young lawyers and aspiring leaders.

Ketanji's leadership extends beyond her professional achievements. She is also known for her commitment to community service and her efforts to inspire young people, particularly women and minorities, to pursue their goals and make a difference. Her public speeches and advocacy work reflect her belief in the power of education, perseverance, and the importance of giving back to the community.

Key Themes and Ideas

One of the primary themes of this chapter is **the power of perseverance.** Ketanji's journey to the Supreme Court was marked by numerous challenges and setbacks, but her determination and resilience enabled her to overcome obstacles and achieve her goals. Her story serves as a reminder that perseverance is a crucial component of effective leadership and that setbacks should be viewed as opportunities for growth and learning.

Another key theme is **the importance of integrity and ethical leadership.** Throughout her career, Ketanji has demonstrated a commitment to fairness and justice, even when faced with difficult decisions. Her leadership is characterized by a strong sense of ethics and a dedication to doing what is right, which serves as an example for others in positions of power.

Additionally, **mentorship and empowerment** are significant themes in Ketanji's leadership approach. She has been an advocate for supporting and guiding the next generation of leaders, particularly those from underrepresented backgrounds. Her efforts to mentor young lawyers and inspire future leaders reflect her belief in the importance of investing in others and helping them reach their full potential.

Critical Analysis

Ketanji Brown Jackson's leadership style provides valuable lessons in **ethical decision-making and advocacy**. Her career highlights the importance of standing firm in one's principles and making decisions that align with one's values. Her example challenges leaders to consider not only the immediate outcomes of their decisions but also their broader impact on justice and equity.

Moreover, Ketanji's approach to **mentorship and empowerment** underscores the need for leaders to actively support and uplift others. Her efforts to mentor young people and promote diversity in the legal profession demonstrate a commitment to creating opportunities for future generations. This aspect of her leadership challenges the notion that leadership is solely about individual achievement and emphasizes the importance of fostering talent and potential in others.

Ketanji's experience also highlights the **challenges of leadership** in high-stakes environments. Balancing personal values with professional responsibilities can be difficult, and her career demonstrates how leaders can navigate these challenges while maintaining their integrity. Her story provides a nuanced perspective on the complexities of leadership and the importance of staying true to one's principles.

Reflective Questions

1. How has Ketanji Brown Jackson's perseverance contributed to her success as a leader?
2. What role does integrity play in Ketanji's leadership style, and how can it be applied in other leadership contexts?
3. How has Ketanji's commitment to mentorship and empowerment influenced her approach to leadership?
4. In what ways can leaders use their influence to inspire and support the next generation of professionals?

5. What lessons can be learned from Ketanji's experience about balancing personal values with professional responsibilities?

Practical Applications

Ketanji Brown Jackson's leadership journey offers several practical lessons for aspiring leaders. First, her example underscores the importance of **perseverance and resilience.** Leaders can apply this lesson by developing a mindset that views challenges as opportunities for growth and by staying committed to their goals even in the face of adversity.

Second, Ketanji's focus on **integrity and ethical decision-making** provides a framework for leaders to follow in their own careers. By prioritizing fairness and justice, leaders can build trust and credibility with their teams and stakeholders.

Finally, Ketanji's commitment to **mentorship and empowerment** highlights the value of supporting and developing others. Leaders can implement this lesson by actively seeking opportunities to mentor and guide emerging talent, promoting diversity, and creating inclusive environments.

Character Profiles (if applicable)

- **Ketanji Brown Jackson:** A trailblazing leader known for her commitment to justice, integrity, and mentorship. Her leadership style reflects her dedication to ethical decision-making and her focus on empowering the next generation of leaders.
- **Young Lawyers and Aspiring Leaders:** Individuals who have been inspired by Ketanji's example and who benefit from her mentorship and advocacy.

Their stories reflect the impact of her leadership on future generations.

Author's Vision and Purpose

In this chapter of *Lovely One*, Ketanji Brown Jackson aims to share the leadership lessons she has learned throughout her career. Her goal is to provide readers with practical insights and inspiration that they can apply to their own leadership journeys. By highlighting her experiences and values, Ketanji hopes to empower future leaders to pursue their goals with integrity and perseverance.

Key Quotes and Insights

- "Leadership is not just about achieving your own goals; it's about lifting others up and creating opportunities for those who come after you."

- "Perseverance in the face of adversity is what separates successful leaders from those who give up too soon."
- "Integrity is the foundation of effective leadership. It's not always easy, but it is always necessary."

Personal Takeaways

Readers of *Lovely One* will gain valuable insights into effective leadership through Ketanji's experiences. Her story offers practical lessons on perseverance, integrity, and mentorship, providing inspiration for those who seek to make a positive impact in their own careers and communities. By applying these lessons, readers can develop their own leadership skills and contribute to a more just and equitable society.

Action Steps and Implementation

To apply the leadership lessons from Ketanji's experience, readers can focus on developing their own **resilience and perseverance** by setting clear goals and staying committed to them despite challenges. They can also prioritize **ethical decision-making** by aligning their actions with their values and principles. Additionally, readers can seek out opportunities for **mentorship and empowerment**, both by finding mentors who can guide them and by offering support to others in their professional communities.

Final Reflections

Ketanji Brown Jackson's leadership journey provides a powerful example of how perseverance, integrity, and mentorship can shape a successful and impactful career. Her story offers valuable lessons for aspiring leaders and serves as an inspiration for those who seek to make a difference in their own fields. Through her commitment to justice and her focus on empowering others, Ketanji demonstrates the qualities that define effective and transformative leadership.

Further Reading and Resources

- *Dare to Lead* by Brené Brown
- *Leaders Eat Last* by Simon Sinek
- *The 7 Habits of Highly Effective People* by Stephen R. Covey
- Articles and case studies on leadership and mentorship.